# Crossing the Bar

## A Professional Fisherman's Tale

by

Joyce Lange Cowen

Nenge Books

**Crossing the Bar - A Professional Fisherman's Tale**
by Joyce Lange Cowen

Published by Nenge Books, Australia, February 2024
ABN 26809396184
nengebooks1@gmail.com
www.nengebooks.com

Design and desktop by Nenge Books

ISBN 978-0-6459597-3-4

# Contents

*To Geoffrey, Julie and Ruth.*
*In memory of your Dad, David Cowen, who left*
*a legacy of love and devotion for all of us.*
*Joyce Cowen.*

# Foreword

Commercial fishing has been a significant industry up and down the east coast of Australia since early settlement, and no more so than out of Iluka and Yamba, on the north coast of NSW, where the Clarence River meets the sea.

Whenever weather and sea conditions permit, trawlers navigate their way across the treacherous bar and out to their fishing grounds.

Joyce Cowen and her husband and family have been part of this fishing community for many years, with lots of adventures and stories to recount. Joyce has combined a number of the true stories and recounted them in this fictional tale of a professional fisherman and his family. It gives the reader a great insight into the practicalities of professional fishing, as well as the dangers.

# A Birthday Party

Most of my birthdays have passed quietly. Just a cake, a coke, a few birthday cards and a dozen or so birthday phone calls. But not this one.

Today is my ninetieth birthday and all my family are here. There's fortyfive of them, counting all the in-laws and out-laws of course. They seem to think that I am special, perhaps they believe that I am getting close to my journeys end. Well!! Each birthday brings the end of this life, plus the beginning of the next life, closer.

Molly and I had two children of our own. However, Molly took on a nephew, a niece and her Dad and cared for them all. We later adopted Annie when she was a baby.

We had just finished a scrumptious meal prepared by my two daughters and granddaughters. As I arose from my chair a voice called out - one of the youngest ones.

"Hey! Gramps, there are more festivities for you! You can't go and lay down just yet!"

Ahh, that was Jack! The cheeky one who comes to visit me more frequently than the others do. He loves to listen to my fishing stories or tall stories. I occasionally have to say to him, "Scamper off Jack, it's time for my lie down."

# The Hat

Grandson Phil brought me a gift in a box and said, "Open it up Grandpa, we want you to try it for size."

When I removed the lid, there nestled amongst the tissue paper was a Sea Captain's Cap. I was too flabbergasted to speak I would have bought one for myself years ago but felt it would make me look too ostentatious. I am a quiet guy and didn't want to be too conspicuous.

The crowd all clapped and hooray-ed, calling out with gusto, "Happy birthday, Captain Grandpa."

As I tried the cap for size, they could see by my smiling face that the gift pleased me. So, I responded by saying, "Thank you one and all very much, you could not have given me a more wanted gift."

"Now then Gramps, don't get a swelled head or the cap won't fit you," came one cheeky voice!

Yes! That was Jack. He always makes me smile. I'm blessed to have a great grandson like Jack. I get such a kick from his expressions. Some may call him cheeky, but I say he's entertaining.

Silver Sea crossing the Bar

# Trip to the Wharf

Son Jake approached me carrying a blindfold.

"Of all things," I said as he tied the blindfold over my eyes. "What a stupid thing to do, I could trip over and break my neck." That would be the beginning of the end. I quietly submitted and was escorted outside and into the utes, with Jack's voice ringing in my ears.

"Good on yer Gramps, keep everyone happy." That's Jack again being his usual self - helping everyone to be happy and in a party mood.

Most of my sons and grandsons have similar voices and they have names I'm familiar with. However, the great grand-daughters names must have been invented, as I've not heard any of them before, some are even unpronounceable!

There was an aura of expectancy and I could hear the excitement in the great grandson's voices. Their rhetoric was louder than usual as we drove away with all the other vehicles following us. We had just passed Shark Bay and I could smell the seaweed. We must be going to Iluka - can't trick an old salt like me.

We soon arrived and slowed down to drive onto the wharf. Jake removed my blindfold and said, "Take a look at this trawler Dad."

I heard young Jack in the background call out. "Get an eye full of this boat Gramps." Jack had a fisherman's drawl even at the age of nine.

# On Board the Boat

Jake helped me onto the wharf and removed the blindfold.

There before my eyes floated a large, new trawler. Everyone on the wharf clapped and cheered.

"Who owns this beauty and how big is it?" I asked.

I was wide-eyed when Jake told me that the three grandsons, Lawry, Clarrie and Phil, were the owners. I could tell that they were very excited about owning such a large and powerful trawler and were anxious to take it to work.

"Take me on board, Jake," I insisted. As the grandies lifted me onto the boat, more cheering echoed from the crowd on the wharf. I must have had an expression of amazement on my face!

"Fancy the family owning a trawler of this size," I said. Jake took me inside the wheelhouse and there in front of me was the most sophisticated technology I had ever seen on a trawler. "Look at this bridge, someone will have to give me the run down on all this technology."

The boys were trying to give me an explanation for each piece of equipment, but I couldn't understand them as they were all trying to talk at the same time.

"Hold it!" I said, "just let Jake explain it all to me." I will admit to being a little deaf.

# *Technology*

It all seemed so complex and confronting.

"I would never be able to sort all this out," I said.

Jake started to explain. "Remember when you had to retire? We were working your old boat. All this complex gear was being introduced onto the trawlers and we skippers had to go to Ballina for lessons. Then later we travelled to Brisbane for exams. That was when we learnt to use this collection of new technology."

"Yes, on recollection, I do remember, most of you were too tired to work and missed a pretty penny on those following nights," I replied.

"Well Dad, every skipper had to know how to use these computers. Being able to plot and save fishing grounds means we can hopefully have better catches. Most fishermen are getting into larger boats now", said Jake, continuing with his explanation.

I listened wide eyed and open mouthed. I didn't want to miss any of the instructions. I anxiously asked Jake the size of the vessel again. He said it was 18 metres long and approximately 6-7 metres wide, a very stable boat which would not roll over easily. The engine was 300hp equal to 200 kilowatts at top speed. Trawling was at 2 ½ knots but top speed was 9 knots.

Jake then began to explain the names of each technical part and how each one was implemented. He explained what the compass was for – of course I knew that already.

"It faces north, gives direction and all positions are marked from here."

"I do know that much."

"Okay Dad. The engine engages the gears and throttle controls. You know that too don't you Dad?"

"Yes! Yes !" I said.

"The echo sounder measures the depth of the water, where you are now. You had one on your old boat as well," Jake continued to explain. "The radar shows above the water and measures distances of objects. This will show up on the radar screen. Are you following me Dad ?" questioned Jake.

I replied, "So far so good."

My comprehension was starting to slow down but I didn't want to admit it. I've noticed that lately information was harder to absorb and I didn't seem to be able to retain it.

Jake continued. "Then there is the track and chart plotter which shows where the vessel is as you steam out to sea. All the tracks show up visually on the computer screen. Okay Dad?"

"Okay," I replied.

"The VHF - very high frequency radio - keeps boats in touch with each other and the Coast Guard. A 'MayDay' call enables every floundering boat to know that help is on the way."

"Okay Pop," said Jake. "How about I take us all out over the bar? I'll start the engine, you take the wheel and steer us down river and over the bar."

I was in my element. This is a beauty to manoeuvre. I felt so proud of my great grandsons. They must have saved much of their wages to achieve so much. This trawler is one to be proud of.

## Vitus Sinks

A little over half an hour of cruising along and my old legs began to tremble. I asked Jake to take the wheel. Before Percy escorted me down the ladder into the fo'c'sle, I asked if I could inspect the engine room. It was spotless. Jake definitely had an interest in this trawler. He was particular, like Molly was.

The fo'c'sle is below deck and it is equipped with bunks and all bathroom necessities. After I lay down, sleep took over and I dreamt about the 'Vitus', my first trawler.

A skipper named Neil helped me bring it home from Queensland and he worked it from Iluka for me. I went back home to the farm to wrap up all the loose ends from the sale.

Vitus 1962

One morning 'Molly' received a phone call from Neil to say the trawler had sunk. Molly laughed, thinking Neil was joking. Nothing to laugh about, this is fair-dinkum! She called me as quickly as she could and, in a return phone call to Neil, he related the story to me.

Apparently the rope that Neil had tied the boat up to the wharf with was too short and as the tide rose the bow of the 'Vitus' became caught under the wharf filling it with salt water. Eventually it sank.

Neil had to pump out all the water and then he asked some of the other fishermen to tow the vessel from where it was and get it onto the slip so he could survey the damage while he waited for me to arrive and decide what to do next.

This was a costly exercise. Everything had to be replaced, not to mention the lost work while the repairs were being made. Fortunately the boat was insured so most of the expenses were covered, but the lost fishing time meant no cash flow. Luckily Molly's Dad was happy to help out.

Vitus being refloated, 1962

## Insured Vitus

We were ready to set sail again. During the time the repairs to the boat were being made I took some time off. I wondered if I had made a wrong decision in selling the farm and changing my occupation.

When the 'Vitus' was back in the water ready for work I drove down to Iluka and became the deckhand on my own boat, so I could learn how to run it by doing and observing.

I remember one particular night so well! The skipper and I hauled in the catch. It dangled overhead in the cod end and Neil went back into the wheel-house to control the steering wheel and keep the trawler on course. I was alone on the deck and without warning and to my surprise the cod end swung my way and knocked me overboard. What a shock! It didn't take me long to see a rope dangling over the side of the boat, which I grabbed and quickly pulled myself back on board. Then continuing to work I pulled the string on the cod end and all the catch fell onto the sorting tray.

The skipper was unaware of my accident. I was too stunned to speak when later I was told sharks always follow trawlers because of the tasty waste which is thrown overboard - unsaleable fish, jelly fish and weed. I was a very lucky deckhand - the sharks missed a healthy meal! I shudder to think about what might have happened to me that night.

All this happened so long ago, couldn't believe I was dreaming about the 'Vitus' and my early experiences. It must have been sixty years ago.

As I slept on more dreams swept over me and I dreamt of a dear friend's demise. I often wished that I could forget the trauma of those times.

Silver Sea trawling

# *Karriss*

*I* was anxious to steer this beauty.

"I forgot to ask, what did you name this boat?" I asked.

"The Karriss," answered Phil. "Remember Grandad, that's the name Grannan wanted you to name the boat you had built in Ballina. You said no one will know what that name means. She said it will be fun to keep the fishermen guessing. 'Karriss' means graceful and beautiful."

She sure is! Looks like a 'white princess' cruising along. I can see her reflection in the river.

Phil was always the closest to Grannan 'Molly', and he was very attached to her. I named my boat 'Matilda'. However it was great that Phil remembered.

The sea ahead was as calm as a millpond. The water was muddy as we had received a few hundred mil's of rain. We would have a trawl on the way back. It was after 1pm now and it would take about an hour to steam far enough to catch a good amount of prawns on the return journey. It which would take 3-4 hours trawling and we should have enough prawns to feed every one of the party people.

We were only trawling with one net to try the trawler out. However, the boys knew the Karriss would have enough horsepower to tow triple gear. Triple gear takes many hours to rig up but is easier to trawl with than double gear, which tangles easier than triple gear. Double gear is towing two nets and triple gear is three nets, but you can catch many more prawns in the same amount of time.

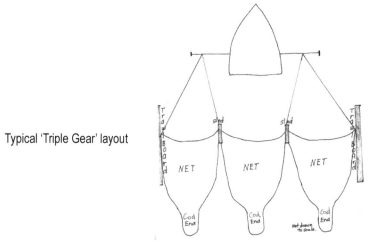

Typical 'Triple Gear' layout

## Tommy Townsend

After taking the Karriss out over the bar, we picked up speed, travelling up to 9 knots. It would take us about an hour of steaming to reach the trawling grounds. To catch prawns, the heavy gear is lowered to the bottom of the ocean and is dragged along the seabed, and the boat's speed is reduced to 2 ½ knots.

I had another rest and dreamt of other happenings to fishermen. Jake said he would wake me when the gear was ready to cast away. This I had to see, as I slowly dozed off.

My thoughts were on the many fishermen who perished. I thought of Tommy Townsend. One Christmas his Mum packed his lunch and he set off to work, buying a carton of cheer as he passed 'Sedgers Reef'. We watched Tommy's trawler disappear out over the horizon, never to be seen again. Not one plank of his trawler was washed up on the beach. We often wondered if the boat ran out of fuel or if pirates attacked him, stealing his boat. We have never to this day heard why he didn't return. His mother waited for him to come home for many months. He was her youngest child.

Before I was awakened I dreamt about another fisherman's demise.

A Yamba fisherman, Billy Venn, was looking through his binoculars when he spotted a small trawler trying to cross the dangerous bar. After twenty minutes or so he decided to steam out to help. The sea was as rough as I had ever seen. No one in their right mind would attempt to make that crossing.

As Molly and I watched from our home - we had a great view of the sea from where we lived. As we looked through our binoculars, the Yamba fisherman was trying to get a rope onto the troubled boat. They both appeared to be in trouble now! Suddenly the boat from Yamba disappeared. A huge wave had swamped his trawler and he drowned. However, his deck hand was washed overboard and was rescued from the Iluka wall.

Most fishermen will help their mates when they get into trouble at sea. Most take risks at their own expense and this fisherman was one of those caring guys. He didn't have to try to rescue the fisherman in trouble and cross that dangerous bar but he did and lost his own life because he cared.

The community were stunned and overwhelmed by the loss of life and the bravery of one of their own. A plaque near the Iluka Co-Op has the names of all the fishermen who have perished at sea as a reminder that the ocean is to be respected.  It can take a life in a few minutes. A fisherman must always be vigilant while at sea.

# Cat Fish Sting

The deckie and I were trawling for school prawns. The weather was perfect and the catch was plentiful. We had never seen such a huge amount of prawns. This was promising to be a wonderful season with such large quantities around the bar. If the weather held calm and the sea so tranquil we would pay off our debts for the season. The river fishermen were catching heaps.

We had just hauled in our last catch of the day and I was merrily sorting without my gloves when - bang !! A catfish spiked me. Oh!! the pain! It went on for hours. The deckie, Bert, insisted that I place my arm in iced water. I hate cold anything but on his insistence I capriciously succumbed to his advice. Yes, it helped. When I removed my arm the pain increased, so I kept it on the ice. Bert fossicked around in the cupboard and found some pain tablets.

"Try these," he said.

After some time the pain eased but I felt giddy and had to lay down. Thankfully the trawler was equipped with a First Aid kit for this kind of emergency. I decided to buy another box of pain killers to replace those I had swallowed. They were prescription drugs and a trip to the doctor was now required.

# Schoolies

On reflection another episode came to my mind as we set out to trawl just off the bar.

It was a beautiful calm morning. We were rigged up to catch schoolies (school prawns). The nets need to be a smaller gauge than for kingies (king prawns). We hauled in after less than an hour trawling and wow, what a catch! We estimated that the shot was about a thousand pounds of prawns.

We winched in the net and emptied the cod end onto the sorting tray. It was chock-a-block full to the top. We would have to head back to the co-op to unload as the icebox would be full and wouldn't hold any more prawns. Harry and I were thrilled. When we reached the wharf Harry started to sort the prawns and I went home on foot and drove Molly back to help. We sorted as quickly as we could, unloaded and steamed back out over the bar hopefully for another thousand, which would take less than an hour. Old Harry looked a little bewildered but cheered up a little when the cod end again held another thousand pounds.

By this time many of the other fisherman had heard about our catch and headed out across the bar to try their luck.

Molly often had hay-fever attacks which caused an itchy nose. She said humorously to Harry, "What do I do when my nose itches?"

"Put up with it," Harry exclaimed angrily.

Molly was speechless and indignant over his angry reply. Later she saw the amusing side of his remark, knowing poor old Harry was absolutely exhausted.

Harry was well past retiring age but needed to work because he had a small daughter to care for. This amount of school prawns were caught before decimal currency was introduced in 1966.

Drew Cason on Ocean Harvester 1996

# Fishing Life

"Time for a cuppa Dad!" shouted Jake, waking me suddenly from my vivid dreams. He helped me up the stairs and I sat on the wheel house bunk and drank a refreshing cup of tea.

"We still have to steam a little further before we drop the gear to catch the prawns for the party on the way back," he said.

After drinking my cuppa I lay down again on the upstairs bunk and would you believe I succumbed to sleep again. It was only to be a short nap but I still dreamt of my fishing days from long ago.

The fishing industry is one of the most enjoyable occupations on earth and sea, but it is not every one's cup of tea nor for the faint hearted. One has to be strong, resilient and eager to work. A fisherman needs to be able to sleep at any time of the day or night. This can be a problem with some young guys. However, I could go to sleep anywhere, at any time. I'd not suffered from sea sickness after only a few trips out to sea to work. This causes a problem with some fishermen who have to employ a skipper and find work to compensate for having to pay the entire crew.

A fisherman's life on the high seas is both enjoyable but dangerous. When speaking to a professional, he has many incidents to recall. Each of these could have been to his demise, however they had the knowledge and expertise to avoid any real disaster. One must know his trawler and keep a proper lookout at all times. It is a safe place if all rules are followed and an alluring way of life to earn a living.

I settled down to trawler work and all it had to offer within a few weeks, for which I am very thankful to God.

When I reflect on my younger days, I remember

encouraging the deck hand to steer the trawler home, which would give him confidence.

So after tidying up the deck, I would sit observing the rising sun. I enjoyed this  tremendously. The golden glowing sun as it slowly appeared was glorious to behold. The calmness and freedom of the voyage home was sublime. I dozed off and was feeling refreshed when we arrived at the wharf ready to unload. The reward would be that the deckie and I knew there would be a good pay cheque at the end of the week.

Wayne Cason on Fleetwing

## Sam & Glenn

I woke but lay there contemplating the past and remembering my good friend Glenn - such a tragedy! Glenn and his son Sam went to work about 2 pm one afternoon. Glenn usually stayed at sea trawling for a couple of nights, coming back to port the morning of the third day.

On the second day, his wife, Janet, could not raise him on her 2-way radio so she asked the other fishermen to call him up.

There was no answer, so most of the fishermen started to search for his trawler. There was no trace. Most of them gave up and those of us who prayed, were praying in an all night vigil.

One morning a few days later I decided to cruise out to where he usually worked and trawl the distance, plus a little wider. Perhaps he and his son had lost radio contact. We just couldn't believe they and the boat had just vanished.

A small object appeared on the screen. I spied something floating and throttled towards it hoping there was signs of life on board. I soon reached it. There was Sam, Glenn's son floating on his inflatable raft. As my deckie and I hauled him on board my boat, we could see he was very dehydrated, sun burnt and nearly incoherent. We called an ambulance and informed Glenn's wife. We did not search any more, we had a very sick young man on board and needed to get him to hospital as quickly as we could.

Sam was taken to hospital and recovered. Between sobs of anguish and despair Sam reported how a large cargo ship had gone off course and ploughed straight into their trawler, which sank on impact. Glenn went down with the trawler and Sam who was on the deck was thrown overboard. Sam was hopeful that Glenn had somehow jumped overboard and that his Dad may have been picked up earlier.

He had managed to climb into the dingy, which stayed afloat for three days, keeping him from drowning. It was a blessing that Sam was a strong swimmer and able to reach the dinghy. All trawlers are equipped with one of these for such an occasion as this. Not all fishermen can swim. Also there had been no time for Glenn to make a MayDay call.

I felt stunned. Glenn's demise took the wind right out of my sails. My heart ached for the family. There was no trawler and no Dad to earn a living. Their livelihood was snatched away in an instant because of the recklessness of a container ship captain.

Geoff Cowen 1978

# Reflections

*I* again began thinking back over the years of my fishing days. I thought about the time of Glenn's demise. I had not thought of him for a while now, his sons had all grown up and had families. His wife Janet remarried and was happily settled in her new life.

I felt stunned. We trawler men must be more vigilant. Glenn was my closest friend. Wasn't it a blessing that Sam was able to swim?

At this time, despair and grief overcame me.  Also fear, it could have been my trawler and me. The bottom seemed to fall out of my fishing life. However, time heals. The trauma eased but I decided to be less blasé when operating my boat. Fear was never an issue at work and I always enjoyed every moment.

So now I told myself I must be more cautious and keep a watch for larger ships which are supposed to steam much further out to sea. The Captain who hit Glenn's trawler was well off course. We fishermen often think we and our trawlers are indestructible. We sometimes take risks. We need to seek God's guidance and pray for each other's safety.

God is our strength in times of peril. We need to remember to pray for God's love and protection every time we go to sea to work.  God's love endures forever.

# Excitement on the Bar

As I lay on the bunk the memories came flooding back. I must have fallen  asleep again and dreamt of another experience.

There had been rough and windy weather and it had lasted for such a long time, six to seven weeks. Now it was slowly abating so we decided to check the bar. The accounts had to be paid and my account at the grocery store was building up. Mr Brimms carried a debt for many fishermen. I hated owing money. Rough seas – no work- no money!!

As we approached the bar the waves were larger than anticipated. Suddenly a huge rogue wave rose up directly in front of the bow. We were tossed so high. I hung onto the steering wheel. This would be a tricky one to manoeuvre! The boat rode it to the top, the bow fully out of the water, then twisting us sideways, heading us for the breakwall. I negotiated it full throttle. I tightened my grip on the steering wheel. The 'Fleetwing' was no match for the force that came heading towards us. (See the photo on the front cover). The next thing I knew we were in calm water heading back up the river. My hands ached from holding the wheel so tightly throughout the drama - I dared not to let it go!

This experience reminded me much of the vigilance we fishermen need to be with the mighty sea.

'Fleetwing' heading back upriver having been turned 180° by a rogue wave.

## Photographer on the Wall

The afternoon the rogue wave hit our boat it was unbeknown to us that this event was going to be recorded and have an impact on the local community.

As our trawler went through its antics when tossed by the rogue wave, there was a photographer on the Yamba wall. He photographed the incredible sequence of twist and turns as the boat was tossed high then smashed back down into the water.

The photographer was ecstatic. He never thought he would capture such an amazing event on camera. He hurried home to have the shots developed, hoping they would capture the drama he had witnessed. When they were printed they were stunning.

The photographer was amazed that the collection of photographs would be so popular, making him a substantial amount of money. They were sold to restaurants, fish and chips shops and displayed in business offices as well as being used as advertising on billboards. Some were even used in marine magazines. They are reproduced here with his permission.

## After Terror on the Bar

After that incident my face lost its look of calm consolation. I think my hair had stood on end as well. My face was frozen and I had been stricken with fear. This had been my first very dangerous episode. From now on we would be more alert to what the sea had to throw at us.

I thought about the plaque at the co-op and all the names of the fishermen - at least ten, who had lost their lives while working at sea. This reminded me that while the sea is awe inspiring, it can take a life in a few minutes. I didn't want to have my name added to the plaque.

I awoke feeling anxious after recalling what I had endured in my dream, and just lay there reminiscing of other much happier experiences.

My son and I mostly trawled for king prawns however there were times when the king prawns were sparse. We needed to try our hands at trapping for Snapper fish. These sold well at the markets. There was also fish like John

Dory, Leather Jackets as well as Snapper to be caught in the traps. They were saleable too. I'm colour blind so red flags were replaced with bright orange enabling me to see where the traps were located. Molly was able to find some very strong gold coloured cotton cloth which she made into flags as markers.

The fish traps were hand made by making a large wooden frame and then covering it in chicken wire, secured by nails. Fish skeletons were used inside the trap for bait, enticing the fish into the traps. These were very long days as we had to steam out to sea for miles. We came home very tired.

But next day when we heard of the weight of the catch, we knew a hefty cheque would be ours. There was a time when we trapped for crayfish. They were also great money spinners.

Life Line on dry dock

The deck hands job is to help and learn from the skipper at sea as well as doing on-shore work. This involves repairing torn nets, maintenance and repairs to the engine and other areas on the trawler. The deck hand is mostly keen to learn all aspects of running a boat so that he will eventually be able to become a skipper himself.

Every three months a trawler is required to be pulled out of the water using the slip so it can be inspected, and the below water area repainted. The above water timbers need to be repainted each year. There is always shore work to be done!

# Molly and Phil

It was a very sad time when we lost Molly.

Phil was very attached to 'Gran-nan' as he named her. He loved to tease her and sneaked the hot baked biscuits she left to cool on the window sill. She would chastise him soundly. He would run off calling, "It wasn't me, it was the magpies you feed. They think you cook the biscuits just for them. Gran-nan you spoil them!"

When Molly passed away Phil was inconsolable. He fretted for quite ,a while. However after a few months he started to play outside with his brothers and mates, but avoided Molly's kitchen for ages. Eventually he recovered.  Molly was with us one day and gone the next. No one had expected her to leave us in her early seventies.

The family was incomplete without her.

# Education

I had a little more education than most of the fishermen. There were two or three I knew who were educated up to Year 12 at High School. However as the years go by one learns from observing, paying attention, and memorising what we see. There are many skills a fisherman needs to learn. Most important is how to deal with break downs. One needs to know how to fix or to recognise just what is wrong with the motor when the boat breaks down. There is also welding, mending nets and how to wrap a wire rope. Operating the electronics is essential in this age of technology. Mobile phones and Facebook have their uses. Looking at the weather forecast before going to sea to work can save your life.

It is the Skipper's duty to teach the deckie if he shows any sign of interest in or obtaining knowledge of how to skipper a trawler. A deck hand needs to clock on when leaving for work and clock off when finishing work. Time at sea is counted before a licence is given. Many hours of trawling time in fact!

When I bought my first trawler I only needed to buy a fishing and boat licence, but these days one needs net licences as well. Much money is spent on all these plus all the gear that has to be rigged up on the trawler first before one can actually work the boat.

My son Jake did not take long to remember and to store all the knowledge he learned. He remembered from year to year where he caught large amounts of prawns. He could tell you where he caught them, the amount, and what the moon phase was. Although he kept a log book he didn't need to refer to it very often. He took to fishing, like a 'duck takes to water.'

To this day Jake is asked by younger fishermen where's the best place to catch Kingies on this moon?

Silver Sea

## Tossing Gear Away.

"Would you like to come on deck, Grandpa we are about to toss the gear away?" Percy's voice rang out.

"Okay come and give me a hand, I don't want to fall overboard!" This will be exciting, I thought.

Percy let me hold on to his arm while we stepped out of the wheelhouse and he kept me steady while I walked down the deck. I found a seat near the drum and watched the whole procedure. Everything worked like clockwork. We were trawling again - my old days were back. Well, this is how I felt. The thrill, the rocking and swaying of the (chine boat) as we towed the gear hoping for a good catch.

I stayed on deck for a while until one of my grandsons called, "Come back and have another cup of tea Grandpa." I stood up feeling the rocking and rolling of the boat under my feet. I needed to steady myself by gripping the side of the wheelhouse till I reached the door.

Later in the afternoon I lay down again on the wheelhouse bunk and again cogitated on days gone by. I soon dozed off and dreamt of other experiences. Many that I thought were lost in time.

A voice rang out.

Dave Cowen & Anne Lange on Life Line off Woody Point

"Wake up Granddad, we are about to lift the gear".

I sat up and steadied myself as I stood holding onto the bunk before I ventured on to the deck again. I could already smell the catch. It sure took me back to my trawling days. How I loved my work. I was young again. The noise of the winch, cacophony of the sea birds calls, waiting for the first morsel to be thrown overboard, really took me back. I was so excited and didn't notice my weak old legs for a while. I just drank in the thrill of it all.

It was a case of all 'hands on deck'. I was included. The catch would make a great meal for all of us back at the house.

The sorting over, the gear hung up, the prawns were cooked and we were on our way home. This would take about an hour.

"Dad, relax on the wheelhouse bunk again this time and you can come out on deck whenever you feel like it," Jake called. By now I had gained my sea legs and could balance on deck but they were aching and reminded me of my weaknesses.

## Back to Port at the Helm Singing

"Hey Grandpa, would you like to take the steering wheel and steer this beauty home?" called Clarrie.

As I continued steering, I felt I was at the helm in my old fishing days. The screeching of the birds overhead was a joy to my ears, my heart leapt and missed a beat or two as I burst into song. My voice was an ordinary tenor singing voice and the sound seemed to be in rhythm with the cadence of the boat.

We were approaching the bar so Jake gave close attention to my steering. The grandsons enjoyed watching me at the wheel. It was all plain sailing from here.

I was jubilant as I sang with gusto and rejoiced as the family men joined me in song. No one has ever been envious of my croaky tenor voice and with the rise and fall of the boat, my voice was even worse. However my birthday was so euphoric that singing was my only way to express myself in happiness as we all praised the Lord together in song.

*Praise the Lord ,*
*Praise the  Lord*
*Let the earth hear His voice*
*Praise the Lord*
*Praise the Lord*
*Let the people rejoice*
*Oh come to the Father*
*Through Jesus the Son*
*And give Him the  Glory*
*Great things He has done.*

I could see the excited people on the wharf waiting for us, who greeted us with much cheering. Some of the family were there to greet us at the wharf, singing 'Happy Birthday Grandpa'. The great grandchildren could be heard calling out 'Happy Birthday Grandpa!' No one shushed them. Half the enjoyment came from their excitement.

The boy's grandsons unloaded the catch onto the utes, ready to take home for the party.

Mystic at the old Co-op wharf, Iluka

## Ending a Wonderful Birthday.

Jake had phoned ahead and some were watching us from the hill on their binoculars. The girls knew I would be tired and were ready to escort me home. By now I couldn't stand alone and two of the great grandsons escorted me from the boat onto terra firma, which seemed to rock like the trawler.

I know this feeling of rocking will pass by morning. This usually happens to every one when they first go to sea. This is my first trip out there in thirty years as I retired in 1995.

Cameras flashed and photos were taken again as I straightened my special Sea Captain's cap.

The family were all there, well mostly as far as I could see, when we arrived back at the party house.

The crew arrived with the prawns. All the women and girls had been busy preparing more food plus creamy mayonnaise, a prawn rich creamy dip and salads too. Most of the party goers enjoyed the freshly caught prawns. So the party continued. The girls served me a light meal. Edith made a cuppa for me and I was able to eat a piece of delicious birthday cake.

I've had a wonderful day. The only regret was that Molly wasn't here with me to enjoy this special day with the family. I thanked everyone for this exciting birthday. The cameras flashed again.

Finally I pleaded weariness and said goodnight. Then the girls escorted me to my bed. They had placed my Captain's cap on the table beside the bed as a reminder of my days and dreams of the sea. The special love of my large family was very present and a truly wonderful blessing.

There I surrendered to exhaustion as it had been a long day, remembering especially to thank the Lord before I slept.

The End.

# About the Author

Joyce Lange Cowen started writing stories late in life and each day she can hardly wait to pick up a pen and write.

Joyce is now 93 years young and writes many letters to her large family and friends. She does not use a computer as they are not as personal as a hand written letter.

Her first novel, *'Elusive Happiness'*, was written when she was in her late eighties and published in 2020. A second short story titled *'Achievement'* was published in 2023.

This work, *'Crossing the Bar - A Professional Fisherman's Tale'*, began to be written in her 92nd year. The story is based on true family experiences in the fishing industry.

Joyce knows Jesus Christ as her Saviour and her Lord from the early age of 16 and wanted to include Christian expressions in her writings as well. She has noted these words that are very meaningful to her from Billy Graham, the great well-known evangelist. He wrote them in his son Franklin's book called *'Through My Fathers Eyes'*.

*"Do we peer into our hope chest – the Bible - and breathe in the Heavenly Fragrance from its pages."*

Poetry is another literary expression she likes to use as well. Many short lines were written on themes of birthday and Christmas. Joyce was very encouraged that some of her Christmas verses were included on the back of Christmas cards for Crossroads Prison Ministry. This ministry uses Bible based lessons like correspondence lessons to prisoners in Australian and Pacific Islands. These awareness and fund raising cards went Australia wide and some overseas. Much longer poems were written too which are included in a photocopied booklet along with the shorter ones. Joyce has had some of the very short lines and bible verse printed onto stickers to be used on the back of the envelopes of letters and cards she sends to many. So you can see she has continued to use her talents and ideas to better others.

Joyce loves sitting in her favourite lounge looking out through the bay windows and garden and doing things like very colourful crotchet rugs and drawing. Her drawings of recent years have been in graphite, drawing from her imagination. Portraits of imaginary people with a lower border of flowers kept her busy for a while, even exhibiting some as well. Now she is focusing on imaginary flowers and leaves with shading to enhance them greatly. Her latest (2023) is using her shaded drawings along with a Bible verse, framed in colour to be used as a card to send to folks.

Joyce has expressed a dream of seeing some of these drawings as prints to be used perhaps on materials for garments. Some have birds in them also which pleased Dave. It has been great to see her talents being used. In her early years she did porcelain painting and this probably gave her the ability to draw flowers and leaves which enables her to pass the time purposefully as gardening is now difficult. Joyce also enjoys playing many tunes by ear on her piano.

Enjoy your read.